Albert Einstein
CREATIVE GENIUS

By Joanne Mattern and Laurence Santrey
Illustrated by Ellen Beier

SCHOLASTIC INC.
New York   Toronto   London   Auckland   Sydney
Mexico City   New Delhi   Hong Kong   Buenos Aires

ISBN 0-439-80152-4

12 11 10 9 8 7 6 5 4 3 2   5 6 7 8 9 10

Printed in the U.S.A.

First printing, September 2005

CHAPTER 1:
A Wonderful Toy

The five-year-old boy lay in bed, fighting the cold that had kept him there for the last few days. He smiled as his father came into the bedroom. "Look at what I have for you, Albert," Hermann Einstein said, trying to cheer up his son. Mr. Einstein held out his hand. In it was something shiny and round—a magnetic compass.

Suddenly, the sniffles and fever didn't matter to Albert anymore. He was fascinated by the compass his father had given him, especially by the magnetic needle inside. It pointed straight north. And no matter which way Albert turned the compass, the needle still pointed in the same direction—north.

Albert played with the compass until his mother came in and told him he must go to sleep. But even then he kept the compass gripped tightly in his hand. It made him want to know so many things. Why did the needle always point north? Were there other toys like this one? What would they look like?

Albert's parents, Paulina and Hermann Einstein, also had questions. But they were about Albert. Mr. and Mrs. Einstein were worried about their son. Mr. Einstein asked his wife if she thought something was wrong with Albert. After all, the boy had not started to speak until he was more than three years old. Even now, he did not speak very much.

"We must not worry," Mrs. Einstein said. "The doctor examined him and told us there was nothing wrong. Just because he did not speak for so long does not mean he is dull-witted."

Her husband sighed. "Ah, well. We are not geniuses. So our son isn't one either."

Mr. Einstein was wrong. Albert *was* a genius, and in time the whole world would know it.

CHAPTER 2:
A Happy Family

Albert Einstein was born on March 14, 1879, in Ulm, a small town in Germany. His father owned a small engineering business that supplied electrical equipment to customers there.

Mr. Einstein got along well with people. But he was not very good at business. Within one year, the Einstein company failed. Then Mr. Einstein's brother, Jakob, had an idea. Jakob had an electrical supply business in Munich, one of Germany's largest cities. He asked Albert's father to move there and become his partner. Jakob would run the factory. Hermann would deal with their customers.

Life in Munich was good for the Einsteins. Many of their relatives lived nearby. Munich was also a grand place to live. It had fine art galleries, concert halls, an opera house, and libraries. Hermann and Paulina Einstein enjoyed all of this. They loved music, literature, and art.

Hermann and Paulina adored their only son, but Albert was not like other boys. He spent hours playing by himself. Albert was very patient and could work on a project for hours. His mother often found him building huge towers made of playing cards. If the tower fell down, Albert didn't cry. He just picked up the cards and started over.

Albert also loved to read. Unlike many other children, he did not like silly stories. Instead, he only read books that were about serious subjects. Learning new things was Albert's favorite pastime

A year after the family moved to Munich, Mrs. Einstein gave birth to a second child, who they named Maja. Two-year-old Albert was thrilled to have a new baby sister. He loved to watch the nursemaid tend to her. He tickled his sister when she cried and was pleased to see her tears change

into smiles. All through their lives, Albert and Maja were close friends.

Hermann and Jakob Einstein's electrical business was very successful. The two brothers soon built a double home in a suburb of Munich. The home was really two houses with no space separating them. An enormous garden surrounded the home with large trees, play areas for the children, flower beds, and a small pond. The entire property was surrounded by a high wall. It was a wonderful place for a little boy with a big imagination to live.

CHAPTER 3:
Long Walks and Music

The Einsteins were a close family that shared
many happy times together. When Albert was in
his sixties, he spoke fondly of a typical Sunday
in his childhood. The day began with a spirited
breakfast conversation about where to hike.

Mrs. Einstein picked the destination—a village or small town in the countryside near Munich. Then Mr. Einstein chose the route they would take.

Albert and Maja loved to listen to the plans Mama and Papa made: which lake they would stop at, what hills they would climb, and what sights they would see. Mr. Einstein was in charge of finding the "perfect" inn to eat at. It had to be comfortable and serve good food. The Einstein children could never remember a disappointing Sunday outing.

The walks the family enjoyed during Albert's youth gave him a love of the outdoors. As a young man, he continued to take long hikes. As he walked, he let his mind wander. He thought about nature, about time, about space, and about all the mysteries of the universe. The scientific theories that would one day startle the world and make Albert famous were born during these long hikes.

Mr. and Mrs. Einstein also gave their children a great love of music. Mrs. Einstein played the piano every day. She believed that it was important for children to play musical instruments. So, at the age of six, Albert began taking violin lessons.

He practiced at least an hour every day. The music delighted him, and he did his best to play it.

But Mrs. Einstein knew that her son would never be a great musician.

One day, Mrs. Einstein saw her son struggling to play a difficult piece of music. "Albert," she said, "only a few people in the world have that special spark that makes a brilliant musician. But music is also a thing of the heart. I do not play in a concert hall. I play my piano for my pleasure and for the pleasure of my family. For you the violin can be the same—an instrument that brings joy and inner peace."

Albert continued to take violin lessons and practice, even though his playing was just ordinary. Then, when he was thirteen, something special happened.

Albert was practicing a piece of music by the great composer Wolfgang Amadeus Mozart. The teenager studied the musical score and suddenly began to see a pattern as pure as the mathematics he knew so well. It was a marvelous discovery for him. From that moment on, Albert played the violin with a deeper understanding. He also found that playing music relaxed him and gave him pleasure. Music would always be an important part of his life.

CHAPTER 4:
School Days

Albert entered school when he was five years old. Most of the teachers at the school were kind, and the rules weren't too harsh.

What Albert did not like were rough sports and military games. When he was a little boy, his parents took him to see a military parade. They thought he would enjoy the columns of marching soldiers. However, Albert was so terrified when he saw the soldiers that he burst into tears. After his parents brought him home, Albert explained that he thought all those soldiers moving together looked like a giant machine. Albert never forgot his reaction to the parade. Unlike most boys, he did not like uniforms, toy guns, or swords. Even as a child, Albert was a person of peace. He was

to grow into an adult dedicated to the ideals of a peaceful world. In time, these ideals forced him to leave Germany forever.

Young Albert did well in elementary school. When he was seven years old, Mrs. Einstein wrote to her mother in 1886, "Yesterday, Albert got his school marks. Again he is at the top of his class and got a brilliant record."

In 1889, when Albert was ten years old, he entered a secondary school called the Luitpold Gymnasium. In German, the word "gymnasium" refers to a special kind of school with a rigorous academic program where students learn mathematics, science, modern languages, history, and ancient languages such as Latin and Greek.

It does not mean a place where people go to exercise, as it does in English.

Albert did not like the gymnasium at all. The boys in the school had to memorize everything and were rarely allowed to ask questions. Teachers spent the class time lecturing. Students spent the class time writing down everything the teachers said.

At Luitpold, when a teacher called on a student, the boy was expected to answer the question perfectly and in the teacher's exact words. The teachers were very strict.

The students were treated like little soldiers. They had to wear uniforms, stand or sit straight at all times, and march like troops from class to class. When they misbehaved, they were often punished physically.

Quiet, thoughtful Albert did not do well at the school. He disliked memorizing facts and rules. Years later he remembered: "As a pupil, I was neither particularly good nor bad. My principal weakness was a poor memory and especially a poor memory for words and texts."

Albert asked his family questions such as "How does darkness happen?" "What are the sun's rays made of?" "What would it be like to travel down a beam of light?" Finding the answers to these questions was much more interesting to Albert than sitting in a classroom and memorizing dates and facts.

Some of his teachers did not understand that Albert thought differently from other pupils. They simply felt that Albert was a bad student. His Greek teacher told him, "You will never amount to anything." On another occasion, Mr. Einstein asked the school's headmaster, "What profession should Albert consider?" The headmaster replied, "It doesn't matter, Mr. Einstein. He will never make a success of himself at anything." The headmaster could not have been more wrong!

CHAPTER 5:
A Special Friend

Albert often struggled to get along with others in school. What most of Albert's teachers did not know was that the boy was doing advanced work in mathematics by himself. It started when Jakob Einstein gave his twelve-year-old nephew a geometry book. The book gave Albert endless hours of pleasure. Not since he had received the compass as a small child had his mind been so stimulated by anything.

Albert taught himself geometry very quickly. Because nobody told him what to think about the subject, he was free to think for himself. He questioned all the facts in the geometry book. When there were no answers, he figured them out for himself. When there were answers, he figured out if they were true and why they were true.

At about the same time, Albert became interested in another important subject — philosophy. It started when a medical student named Max Talmey became a regular dinner guest at the Einstein home. Each family in the Einstein's neighborhood was responsible for feeding a student once a week. That way, a student without much money did not have to worry about the cost of food that day. A student could eat at a different family's house each day of the week.

Thursday was Talmey's day to eat with the Einsteins. Albert looked forward to Thursdays because Talmey talked to him about science and philosophy. Philosophy is the study of the meaning of life and the universe.

Talmey quickly recognized Albert's brilliance.

The medical student gave Albert very
challenging philosophy books to read. Albert
then discussed them with Talmey. The thirteen-
year-old began to think about things he had
never thought about before. He wanted to know

how the universe operated. He wanted to explore the laws of nature. He wanted to find answers to questions that had puzzled scientists and philosophers for centuries. Albert questioned the accepted ideas of the era. He knew there was more to be learned about space and time.

At the time Albert lived, it was impossible for people to travel to the stars and beyond. The only way to do that was in the mind. And so, Albert started studying the subject that was to become his life's work. He plunged into a type of science called theoretical physics. This science looks at the physical world and tries to make sense of it by using mathematics. Everything on Earth—from small atoms to large galaxies—is studied in theoretical physics.

Max Talmey was deeply impressed by young Albert. Years later, Talmey wrote, "Soon the flight of Albert's mathematical genius was so high that I could no longer follow."

CHAPTER 6:
A New Life

In 1894, the Einsteins' factory closed. This time, help came from a cousin of Mrs. Einstein. The family packed up and moved to Milan, Italy. There, Mrs. Einstein's cousin had opened a branch of the family business and asked Mr. Einstein to run it.

Albert remained in Munich. The fifteen-year-old boy moved into a room in a boardinghouse and continued his studies. His family expected him to finish the school year, get a diploma, and begin university studies. But these plans fell apart not long after the Einsteins moved to Milan.

Although Albert did brilliantly in mathematics

and philosophy, his work was below average in other subjects. He was not liked by his teachers either. Albert often asked questions they could not answer. At times, he even challenged the strict discipline of the school.

Einstein described what happened after his family moved to Munich: "I was summoned by my homeroom teacher who expressed the wish

that I leave the school. To my remark that I had done nothing amiss, he replied only, 'Your mere presence spoils the respect of the class for me.'"

Albert had had enough of the school. He also knew that when he turned seventeen, he would have to join the German army. This was a horrible fate for someone who believed in peace. For these reasons, Albert was happy to leave the school and join his family in Italy.

The next two years were among the happiest of his life. He visited museums, attended concerts, and read everything he could get his hands on. His parents were unhappy that he had left school, but Albert promised that he would keep studying on his own. He had already taught himself a very advanced kind of math called calculus, and had developed a keen scientific curiosity.

Even Jakob Einstein realized just how far his nephew's learning had advanced when young Albert solved an engineering problem that had delayed Jakob in constructing a machine. "You know," he later said to a close friend of Albert's, "it is really fabulous with my nephew. After I and

my assistant engineer had been racking
our brains for days, that young sprig had got the
whole thing in scarcely fifteen minutes. You will
hear of him yet."

During the same two-year period, Albert wrote
his first scientific paper, which he sent to an uncle
back in Germany. The subject of the paper was
the relationship of electricity, magnetism, and
ether. Most scientists of the time believed ether
was an invisible substance. It was said to fill space
and carry electromagnetic waves. Young Albert
was not ready to accept the existence of ether,
which is a kind of gas. He felt that the presence of
ether had not been proven, and he said so in his
paper.

In 1896, seventeen-year-old Albert entered the
Swiss Federal Institute of Technology in Zurich,
Switzerland. He majored in physics and planned
to become a physics teacher. But he soon saw
that the physics being taught at the institute was
out of date. The teachers didn't know it yet, but

Albert's private studies were far more advanced than their own.

Albert graduated from the institute in 1900. Unfortunately, he had to give up teaching. His professors were annoyed because Albert told them that their thinking was behind the times. Not only would the institute not hire him, but it also would not recommend him for a job at any other school. Albert needed to find a different way to earn a living.

CHAPTER 7:
Great Discoveries

Albert had a good friend named Marcel Grossman. Marcel's father helped Albert get a job at the Swiss Patent Office in Bern, Switzerland. Albert was part of a team that examined and recorded applications for patents submitted by Swiss inventors. He worked there for the next seven years. Albert enjoyed his job. He was also happy that it gave him a lot of free time to study physics and mathematics on his own.

The result of this studying was a series of scientific papers. One of them was called *A New Determination of the Sizes of Molecules.*

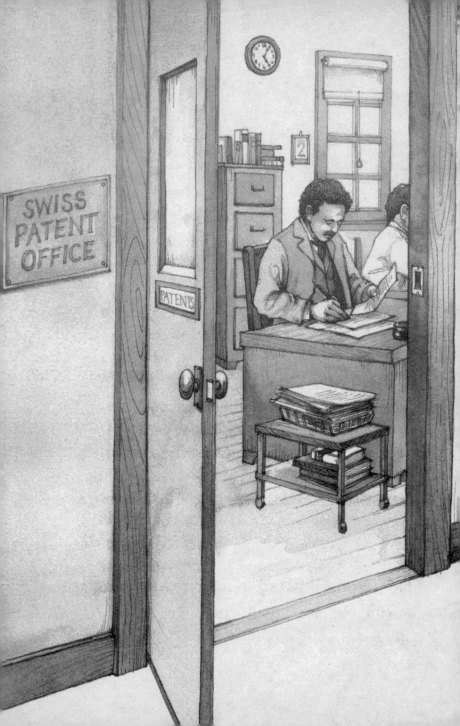

SWISS
PATENT
OFFICE

PATENTS

Albert submitted this paper to the University of Zurich in 1905. At that time, scholarly papers of great merit could be accepted for a Doctorate of Philosophy degree without a student having to go through years of formal classroom study. Einstein's paper was accepted by the university, and he received his degree. With it, he could teach at the university level.

Another paper Albert wrote in 1905 contained his special theory of relativity. This theory is about uniform motion in a straight line, or speed that is constant. For example, suppose you are riding a train moving at a constant speed and you drop a book. The book would drop straight down, not at an angle. You would get the same result if you stood still on level ground outside the train and dropped the book. As long as the train is moving at a constant, or uniform, speed, the book's fall to the ground will not be affected by the train's motion.

Albert wrote other papers that led to the study

of atomic energy. Most of what we know today about atoms and molecules, and the relation of space, time, and the speed of light, comes from the ideas of Albert Einstein.

CHAPTER 8:

"The Greatest Mind of the Twentieth Century"

In 1921, Albert Einstein was awarded the Nobel Prize in Physics. By this time, he was already considered by many to be the greatest thinker of the twentieth century. His ideas had revolutionized science. But they remained theory until World War Two. Only with the first experiments in nuclear fission were Einstein's theories made real.

One result of his work was the invention of the atom bomb, which helped to end World War Two. Other results have been the creation of radiation therapy to cure cancers, the development of the laser, and space exploration.

The last twenty-two years of Albert's life, from 1933 until his death on April 18, 1955, were spent at the Institute for Advanced Study in Princeton, New Jersey. In the quiet college town, Albert was a familiar sight to all. Every day, the kindly old gray-haired gentleman walked from his home to his office. Only when the weather was extremely hot or cold was he willing to travel in a car rather than walk.

The walks were Albert's thinking times. But he was always ready to stop and speak with anyone who approached him. Even though he was widely considered the greatest genius of the twentieth century, Albert talked seriously with anyone of any age. He respected little children as much as the presidents, prime ministers, and Nobel Prize winners who visited him.

Albert never abandoned his other childhood love, music. A number of his

closest friends at Princeton's Institute for Advanced Study were amateur musicians like him. During the day the scientists worked on serious, scholarly problems. At night they played the music of Bach, Beethoven, Mozart, Brahms, and Mendelssohn. And when Albert was finally too old to play the violin, he spent his evenings listening to the records of the music he loved. His mother's gift of music remained one of the delights of his life.

Albert Einstein's work opened up the universe. Today, scientists explore space, the origin of the universe, and the mysteries of the particles that make up the atom. These are studies made possible by the gentle, peace-loving genius, Albert Einstein.